Nobody understands another's sorrow, and nobody another's joy.

FRANZ SCHUBERT

Oh Vienna!
Bellissima Publishing, LLC

Introduction

Vienna, the largest city in Austria, is its capitol. It is known as the city of music because of its musical roots, and it is also known as the city of dreams because it was home to the world's first psycho-analyst, Sigmund Freud. The roots of the city lie in early Celtic and Roman settlements that created a Medieval, Baroque city.

Photographer John D. Weigand and award winning author, attorney and former teacher, Penelope Dyan visited Vienna just before Christmas and saw many things that would delight a child. Dyan believes the key to traveling well with a child, especially a young one, is to not put them into overload. "If you do that," Dyan says, "then all you will end up with are complaints of tummy aches and hurting feet." The trick here is to let the child absorb, because a child is like a sponge. Let them look at pictures and then just watch and see what he or she sees. Museums are soon forgotten, and what is remembered is what they saw as only they can see. Dyan asked a well traveled young Italian child in Spain what he liked to do when he traveled, and he simply answered, "Go to playgrounds and parks." According to Dyan, if you want to see with a child's eyes, ask a child what they see! This is how Dyan sees through the eyes of a child. There is also a video on the Bellissimavideo YouTube Channel that goes along with this book!

Oh Vienna!
Bellissima Publishing, LLC

Oh Vienna!

A kid's Guide To Vienna, Austria

By Penelope Dyan

Oh Vienna has so much
to do and to see!
This Lipizzaner Stallion
was especially appealing to me!
There he stood in a stable
in the middle of the town.
He looked right at me,
and then he looked right down.

* Had it not been for General George S. Patton saving the Lipizzaner breed at the end of World War II from extinction, there would be no Lipizzans today, proving one person can make a difference.

There is a Ferris wheel* round
that will take you up high,
where you can sit in a basket
that touches the sky.

* The 'Giant Ferris Wheel' is open all year round. It is one of the most visited attractions in Vienna. 'Ferris Wheel Square' was redesigned in 2008. The entrance to Prater Amusement Park is a nostalgic theme of 1900.

It was nearing Christmas,
so this corner was lit;
and I wondered at the sight of it.

The unlit lights of day I saw,
will sparkle through the night,
as birds fly through the air,
far away and out of sight.*

* This is another view of Hofburg Palace, a little different from the cover photo, on this book of Hofburg Palace; and as you can see, it is at the end of a busy street.

And in a window there was, I think,
a very fancy cake,
But it was certainly not like anything
that Mom could EVER bake!

The colors in the church* were a feast
for the eyes' delight,
that shown this very day
with the colors of Christmas,
although it was NOT Christmas night.

* This is St. Stephen's Cathedral, and this is where the very famous composer Ludwig van Beethoven discovered the totality of his own deafness when he saw birds flying out of the bell tower as a result of the bells ringing, but could not hear the bells. St. Stephen's Cathedral has 23 bells in all.

And the statue Athena
bathed in gold
told a very poignant story,
of mythical times past,
and the times
of Greek gods' glory.*

* This is the Parliament building and here is the statue of Athena. The main entrance at the portico is an exact copy of the gate of the Erechtheion on the Akropolis in Athens, and it is fitted with a bronze portal.

And among all the music* and the art,
Amadeus Mozart was a part.
You see, in Vienna, everywhere,
the sound of music fills the air.

* Many 18th and 19th century composers came to Vienna due to the patronage of the Habsburgs. They made Vienna the European capital of classical music. Wolfgang Amadeus Mozart, Ludwig van Beethoven, Franz Schubert and Johann Strauss II, among others, created music here; and Franz Schubert was born in Vienna.

On corners and streets,
if you stop and take a look,
are statues so numerous,
they could fill a book.

* This is a rear view statue of Ferdinand Raimund (1790–1836) as he is being looked over by an angel. Ferdinand Raimund abandoned his apprenticeship in a bakery to become an actor. Three of his eight plays are well known, and they are occasionally staged today. They are 'Der Alpenkönig und der Menschenfeind' (The King of the Alps and the Misanthrop), and 'Das Mädchen aus der Feenwelt oder Der Bauer als Millionär' (The girl from fairy land or the farmer as millionaire) and 'Der Verschwender' (The dissipator).

Then there he is, Pinocchio sitting on a bench outside a store.
There are toys inside,
and gifts galore!
You go inside and buy a wooden toy.
Your heart fills with happiness,
as would any girl's or boy's.

And as you look at Mozart,*
(surrounded by a tree
bearing leaves of red)
Your mother reminds you
that it is soon time for bed.

* This Mozart monument stands across the street from the Academy of Fine Arts, located at Burggarten 1010, Vienna, Austria.

Then you see trees of green,
ready for Kris Kringle, it would seem.
And the boys and girls of Vienna
know on Christmas Eve Day,
that old Kris Kringle is on his way.

If life is a dance, you must never let the music stop.

PENELOPE DYAN